Cannibals and Missionaries

Cannibals
and
Missionaries

John Fuller

Secker & Warburg · London

First published in England 1972 by
Martin Secker & Warburg Limited
14 Carlisle Street, London W1V 6NN

Copyright © John Fuller 1972

Designed by Philip Mann

436 16802 2 (cloth)
436 16803 0 (paper)

Printed in Great Britain by
Cox & Wyman Limited,
London, Fakenham and Reading

For Prue

Acknowledgments

Acknowledgments are due to the following, where some of these poems first appeared: *Agenda, Antaeus, The Listener, The New Statesman, The New York Times, The Poem of the Month Club, The Poetry Book Society Supplement, The Review, The Times Literary Supplement* and *Vortex*. Some of the longer poems have appeared in pamphlet form: **The Art of Love** was published by *The Review*, **The Labours of Hercules** by the Manchester Institute of Contemporary Arts, and **The Wreck** by Turret Books. Novello published the **London Songs** and *Herod Do Your Worst* (from which **Lullaby** and **The Father's Song** are extracted) with music by Bryan Kelly.

Contents

The Two Sisters

He saw her fingers in the candlelight
Crooked with the needle, poised to break a thread,
Or at her temple pressed to ease the sight,
With one thin strand of hair loose from her head
Falling in its tiredness, cedar red,
Across the bent and pale half-humorous face,
Hair like a precious garment of the dead
Tucked now behind the ear into its place,
An automatic gesture yet with grace
To make a ceremony of her task
When fingers smoothing down the finished lace
Are answered by the question that they ask
Of labour's quiet satisfaction, such
As simply sanctifies the sight and touch.

That one he loved, the other in a dream
Possessed his spirit, though she never smiled;
One with rolled sleeves or lost in linen's steam,
Fruit in her apron for the orphaned child,
The other walking by herself, beguiled
By passing beggars and by horoscopes;
That home to him, this every day more wild;
One was his shelter, one played out his hopes,
A mind that grasps uncertainty and gropes
For wind-wide vistas from delirious rocks
While others go no further than the slopes
On which they tend the necessary flocks.
Both sisters were his world. From each he learned
What man must die from. And to both returned.

Her sister wasn't helpful, that was certain,
Lying with headaches on her bed all day,
The neighbours wondering at the fastened curtain,
At the strange girl who only knelt to pray
With steps to scrub and the day's fires to lay,
Who stared at breakfast, had no time to spend

In gutting fish and could not see her way
To lay the table for her brother's friend.
The world would take more than one life to mend,
The other thought: there simply wasn't time
To moon about the inevitable end,
For death remained as private as a crime
And as improbable, so long as life
Whitened her knuckles that enclosed the knife.

They told her not to think about the fish.
The fish was simply something they could eat.
It had to die to turn into a dish.
Once dead there was no memory in meat.
She bit her lip, muttered and left her seat,
Her plate untouched. Apologies were made,
A mention of her efforts and the heat:
No wonder nerves were just a little frayed.
But who foresaw as she did death's curved blade
Casting its shadow on the company
And their autumnal guest whose hands displayed
The future's frightening leap, his ruined tree?
Her brother lost to him, white as a sheet,
Her sister still, devoted, at his feet.

And now as if a promise were fulfilled,
Insistently, uncruel, even with joy,
As children tread the towers that they build
And love the crouching cat that they annoy,
Death with his conjuror's fingers took the boy
And left his body still, as one might leave
Forgotten in its box a broken toy.
Mourning has very little to achieve:
A neighbour wiped his eye upon his sleeve
And friends came to console them for their loss.
The sisters found that they could better grieve
If death were seen as swaddling pinned across
His face. They moved their fingers to the brooch
That held it there. Their hope was a reproach.

Death was the knowledge that eluded him,
The senses stunned to feel the body cease,
The spirit sobbing in the missing limb,
The sisters exiled from their brother's lease
And its reversion. In the perfumed peace
Of living's shadow nothing was revealed.
He realized the strangeness would increase
As time unwound its laps about the field
Where he pursued again the power that healed
Its stubborn strokes: those hands laid on his death
Were lent themselves to death and so unsealed
At once his own and every stifled breath
To speak, amazed, of what life was about.
And turned the everlasting inside out.

He was still alive. And the sisters passed
Silently and with great joy into
The landscape of his unbound eyes at last.
One in the wisdom of her insight knew
How life describes its need to be thought true
In terms of its illusions, and she made
Her happiness the air to which she grew.
The other was content to live in shade,
Grew downwards, desperately, undisplayed.
Both were his nature. That he understood.
Perhaps uncertain, even half-afraid
Which to embrace, he knew that both were good,
As on his heel, beneath his wrinkled skull,
Moved the creased sweating happy miracle.

So when the perfume filled the house she smiled
Inside herself. It was the good part. Both
Were good. She was excited as a child
Though busy with preparing food and loath
To leave it. Someone present swore an oath
It would have paid a labourer for a year,
But who could measure growing against growth,
Or time the seed against the waving ear?

And now one knew it, what was death to fear
But this extraordinary ritual where
Its moment was acknowledged to be near,
Its mystery by a sister's healing hair
Divulged? To smile was to betray her sense
Of love in perfume, tears, experience.

Lecture Room: Ten AM

Robed in black, like surgeons already in mourning
For a dramatic failure in our usual techniques,
Amputation of Wordsworth or extraction of impacted Keats,
We hold precious as the last candle carried in cupped hand
The notion that here, at this place and at this time,

The twin tyrants of passage and location with their goads,
The murderous rubato, the spiritual ampallang,
Might for once be cheated of their inevitable victory
And something simple and other, like a flickering flame,
Be held a moment for surprised contemplation.

They are not appeased. Their anchors weigh down hands and eyes
To abject homage before their disgusting achievements.
Amusement, idleness, study: all are irrelevant
Since the black conspiracy equally absorbs them all,
And the life that should be shocked and free is still tame.

The heroes are shown not to falter, or to falter superbly,
And voices from all the rooms rise gradually through the walls
In acknowledgment of the cult which binds us:
'''Tis not contrary to reason to prefer the destruction
Of the whole world to the scratching of my finger.'

'The last passage is not yet sufficiently explicated.'
'No one has ever seen the female palingenia:
Fecundated before even getting rid of her nymph's corset,
She dies with her eyes still shut,
At once mother and infant, in swaddling clothes.'

Examination Room: Two PM

All the ingredients of interrogation, green baize,
Papers strewn with care, faces averted in unconcern,
Impossible questions: these establish and then relax
The identity-conditions. Thus, as colours are real
When we say 'red' and 'yellow', and yet are hard to find

Within such generalities, so the predication of interrogation
Locates the candidate only within those classes of candidate
To which he may with safety be admitted, and today
All the submissive accidentals, fainting, beauty, garrulity
And wrong clothes, are simply the material for anecdotes.

The old hate the young for believing them to be really old.
The young hate the old for knowing that they are in fact young.
Both are dangerously polite. Only these must for the moment suffer:
All aggression, all curiosity, all friendship is put aside.
They weep with gratitude, with laughter and with being hurt.

Upper Reading Room: Six PM

In the guilty half-silence of this long
Waiting-room, allusions buzz for us
Like flies, chairs scrape back for topics leaving
From a different platform. Lugging each hero's baggage,
We lie: 'I am like you. You are alive in me.'

Kipper-tied quinquagenarians, tramps
With satchels, academic teeny-boppers
Their carrels piled with hats and avocados,
Knee-locked civil servants of apparatus,
Nuns: we are shades that have lasted one more day.

And our eyes meet over the low partitions
In tentative love, sharing our furtive sense
Of the insults of that antagonist with whom

We ever contrive grandmaster draws, who sets
The problems that we compromise, from whom

We all on some long morning learned the rules.
He stains the stones. The scaffold streams with him.
Leggy girls on their venerable monosyllables
Are led by him to a gagging dryness. Boys
Smooth their balding heads, invoking his praises.

He brings the wrinkled clean expatriates
To the dug-outs of a mad ambition, shading
Their narrowed eyes on the beaches of exegesis,
Saying: 'We will return.' He likes to see
A gulping of tesseracts and Gondals in

Our crazed search across sands of the impossible
For the undying, and he annotates
Pistacia terebinthus to a sacrament,
Its sweet stench long evaporated
In the pages of a demythologized

Indexed kerygma. But we refuse to be bullied,
Even as hammers slog the walls crumbling
Around us. Books are about life, and life
Is somewhere here. On paper. In eyes. Somewhere.
So now we stack our cards. We reserve our defence.

The Art of Love

Half humanity conspires
To meet the other half's desires.
You may imagine this shows willing,
But every cake must have its filling.
Disheartening demands dishearteners;
The firm of Love is run by partners.
Investing little, you come off it
Quits at least or with quick profit,

But if you risk your only capital
The chances are your Co. will sap it all.
This exploitation has its sequel
In the old myth that girls aren't equal,
That men are fighters for their sakes,
That girls are flowers and men are rakes.
Girls found this easy to accept,
Wilted, and wanted to be kept,
And at the merest hint of violence
Tended to take the Vow of Silence.
Faced with a rape, abject *Clarissa*
Felt that Heavenly Bliss was blisser,
And something of this doubtful truth
Lingered in *Amy*, *Nell* and *Ruth*,
Whose postures are so unromantic
They drive the modern reader frantic.
When the Victorians swapped *Haidée*
For *The Portrait of a Lady*,
Believing Will betrays you rather
Than pressure from an irate father,
Adultery replaced the idyll,
Love was at most a moral riddle,
And tempted *Maggie* found it best
To please *St Oggs* not *Stephen Guest*.
Our sense of outrage comes in handy
But shrinks to disbelief with *Candy*
Whose innocence is half-voulu
As she enacts what not to do,
Whose protest, awe and resignation
Spring from maternal compensation
And yields her Treasure in despite
Of love, intelligence or right.
But literature deceives us yet
With situations never met
In living's zany plotless zoo
Where there's no *she* but only *you*
And consequences not tendentious,
Adventures only half-adventures.

Men are inclined to dream about it
(Even more with it than without it).
No wonder girls now seem remote:
For centuries they've missed the boat.
Daphne addressed by hot *Apollo*
Found sexual stimulation hollow
(A female growing leaves and rigid
Must be symbolic of the frigid).
Some girls think sonnets are more moral,
Withhold their love but grant the laurel,
And men are sometimes pleased with this,
Would rather they admire than kiss.
But who unless he fails his wife
Thinks art has thus the edge on life?
The view was held in some abhorrence
By, among others, *D H Lawrence*,
Who showed a most unseemly hurry
To take it out on *J M Murry*.
Lawrence thought every woman should
Be shown that her desires are good,
That *amor naturale*'s error
Lies in obeying Ego's terror.
Lawrence, too, contrived to train us
In the importance of the anus,
Not *Sade*-like as a matter of course,
But to return us to a Source
Which, with some conscientious plumbing,
Could liberate the Second Coming.
The thing was pointed out by *Sparrow*
Whose verdict though was rather narrow:
It seems because men have them too
That anuses are thus taboo,
As though girls stroking hairy chests
Imagine nipples might be breasts.
Absurd! Ignore all things we share,
There'd be no point in being bare.
This was typical Lawrentian
To hint at things you just don't mention,

Nor for the Warden of *All Souls*
Was it the liberalest of roles
To analyse with strange disgust
What *Lawrence* never said we *must*
But only what we *might* do when
We had to show that we were men.
And if this subject makes you queasy
Remember that the act's not easy
And most perversions are fantastic,
Requiring humans of elastic.
   Some are within the powers of man:
We all can do what someone can.
But are they done? And who can tell?
The secrets starlets try to sell
And every case of liar's quinsy
On his knees to *Dr Kinsey*
Show that there exists in most
Of us a strange desire to boast.
Sex is the one activity
Which doctors aren't allowed to see,
So how on earth can they advise?
What limitations it implies!
Dr Johnson and *Dr Masters*
Excluded obvious disasters,
Turned from their scientific eye
The weird, incapable or shy,
And steered around a public storm
By sticking firmly to the norm.
Yet who if he is really normal
Could stand an atmosphere so formal?
What decent girl would choose how thick
She'd like her perspex camera-prick?
These are reactions of suspicion
Quite natural to observed emission
Since mad desire and blinkered science
Form an impossible alliance:
You can't predict the former's acts,
You can't believe the latter's facts.

B

From all the possible examples
Let's take the way it chooses samples:
As prototype of penises
The statistician favours his:
Smaller, you would not think he lies;
Larger, you've no care for size.
Sexology is not obscene,
Only an interest in the Mean.
Or if obscene it's not absurd:
Today a neutral tone's preferred.
Figures can hardly be converted
To arguments for the perverted
Because the tales are out of school
And flout, not constitute, the rule,
Because the one unnatural act
Is what you can't perform (a fact):
And doctors can't decide for you
The things you should or should not do.
You'll get away with most wild oats,
Liking sheet plastic, doorknobs, goats,
Without the slightest moral qualm
Unless you're doing someone harm.
All this is understood, but what
We publicize it for is not.
Perhaps the purely mental rapes
Of Apollonian sour grapes
Encouraged by retreating from
Daphne's arboreal aplomb
Have lured us all into the state
Of liking love, but not a mate.
Yet does this theory really fit?
And what about it's opposite?
    Man is aghast at woman's claim
When making love to feel the same,
And so he perpetrates the fiction
That passion can dispense with friction,
Bestows divinity on girls
As ermine is passed on to earls.

In turn, he likes to be adored
(The common cause that they are bored);
His weeping makes them powerful
Like tides beneath the monthly pull.
Or he might fail to make love mystic
And try instead to be sadistic,
Taking it where and when he will,
Secure in pleasure and the Pill.
In either case the brute ignores
His elementary sexual chores.
Something is wrong, and it's not theory
That makes a man too quickly weary,
Too prone to boggle or to poke,
To crack the egg but waste the yolk.
It's feminine emancipation
Has led girls to expect elation:
Now nature sparks with one hand all
That with the other she can stall,
And those who'd strike for their orgasm
Suspect a girl who claims she has them.
Lack of feeling's now no shame
Since it's the man they've got to blame:
He's baffled, too, by what's expected,
Like a dictator who's elected,
And the explicitness is gruelling
When he's continually refuelling
For expeditions that are wrecked if
He's told he's missed his prime objective.
True, there are various kinds of guilt
(He cannot help the way he's built)
But is the guilt his always? Would
A different partner do some good?
The girls who are forever trying
May be, with mere frustration, lying,
For even bankers are not candid
When they're discussing the Gold Standard.
It is not seemly to compare,
Comparisons are most unfair.

One shrugs, another says 'It's scrumptious!'
To rave or scorn, both are presumptuous.
There is this myth that girls are seemly,
But really they are not extremely,
And many kinds of dampeners
Are not her partner's fault but her's.
E.g., the Girl You Hate To Love:
She's sure the man must be above,
And has it clearly from a book
That the true *Venus* likes to look,
Then just when you are feeling hot
Sweetly complains that she is not.
Worse is the scientific kind,
Too interested to drop behind,
Too interested to be involved:
It's like a problem to be solved,
Testing with fingers and with thumb
Or asking coolly if you've come.
She likes to state with some precision
The pros and cons of circumcision
Or why whenever she has necked
Her nipples have not been erect.
   This barrier of relished knowledge
Began when girls demanded college,
Last revolutionary straw
Upon a baleful neighing Law
Which had for centuries demanded
That men should govern single-handed
And Married Women's Property
Suffrage, Schools, Equality,
Be subjects on which men should judge:
Women should sew, give birth, make fudge.
Girls once were married off with dowries,
Ten cows or fifty strings of cowries.
Love, starting in the Middle Ages,
Like sin demanded certain wages:
You couldn't keep a wife in service;
Sex and hard work would make her nervous.

So she achieved her own position
And with it came a sense of Mission.
She was a goddess or a wit,
But power did not come into it.
Updating *Shakespeare*'s heroines
Shows how the Nineteenth Century wins
By giving their implicit urges
Explicit shape as power emerges.
Thus *Helena* in horseless carriage
Reclaims with speed her ruthless marriage,
And *Rosalind* politely shows
She knows What Every Woman Knows,
While *Leonato*'s morning coat
Gives *Beatrice* the urge to vote:
Men must retrench, reform, adapt.
Unless they do they're surely trapped.
Now anything the father says
In matrilocal marriages
Shows the reserve of the intruder,
The ironist, the dark alluder
Who manages to squeeze applause
Out of the stoniest of In-laws
By recognition of his lack
Of power to give the whip a crack,
By humorously living down
His soon-accepted role of clown.
So when the man is weak and comic,
The reason must be economic:
The *Longbourn* entail gave the tenet
Of sarcasm to *Mr Bennet*,
Who capped the impotence of *Lear*
By joking with disasters near:
Five daughters and you play it cool,
Witty in storms and your own fool.
A *Lydia*'s content with jollity,
Elizabeth must have equality:
But knowledge is a doubtful sequel
To women's need of being equal;

Incredible a female *Faust*:
Their only aim's to be espoused.
And yet to pass from comic annuals
Overnight to marriage manuals
Gives a girl a certain poise
And wisdom in the ways of boys.
It's surely wrong to say embraces
Made in the forbidden places
Induce in girls unusual fervour:
They're simply primed by The *Observer*,
By Lost Boys chasing frequent thimbles,
By seers with beards and finger-cymbals,
By bottom-filmers and adverts,
By queer designers of short skirts.
   Yet after all the drugs and hope
Girls quickly tread the downward slope
To vales of domesticity
And whether to have Two or Three,
And those who turn to *Dr Spock*
When their first suitor starts to knock
Typify the usual aim
Of those who, married, change their name.
To multiply is to divide
Male cautiousness by female pride:
Until they start to put some flesh on
Or have to think of The Succession,
Men are rarely very wild
To start things moving with a child.
Women, however, disagree.
To them the state of pregnancy
Is something monthly they can measure
More tangible than weekly pleasure,
And giving birth's a giant expulsion
Of every sexual compulsion,
For it's well-known that only whores
Make merry of the menopause.
   Of different ways to gain a bed
It's better that there's little said,

For no one can be sure it's right
To fumble every flower in sight,
And many ways of getting in
Strike one as being ungenuine:
When the erratic secretary
Is working late and offered sherry
The boss with a well-sharpened pencil
Explores the mazes of her stencil;
The student, with a knowing grace,
Achieves the alpha of her face;
While housewives turn up Radio Four
To drown the milkman's happy snore.
Yet even lovely marriages
Can suddenly appear a swizz,
The hairy husband lose his shape,
The willing wife complain of rape;
And often, to compose a rift,
A quarrel's ended by a gift:
There's chilling passion in contrition
When pearls produce a new position.
For love can't bribe or predicate,
Love's a collision not a state,
It isn't only Soft Machinery,
It tends to rumble down like scenery.
There's no advice which can redeem
A symphony without a theme
And even *Raymond Postgate* might
Be lost without his appetite:
Lovers, beware of exercise,
Too many muscles, there's no prize,
No will to Be without belief,
No use in grovelling or grief,
No love without that Accident
Which tells the puppet what it meant,
Descends from its machine and grants
Joy to the Have-nots and the Can'ts,
Projecting in their childish serial
An episode quite immaterial

Which to their endless racked suspense
Answers in the present tense.
Love has no watch, no train to catch,
No lingering, no plot to hatch;
It is the current not the cog,
It is itself, no pedagogue:
Love's unforeseen affirmative
Is all the teaching it can give.

God Bless America

When they confess that they have lost the penial bone and
                                             outer space is
Once again a numinous void, when they're kept out of Other
                                                    Places,
And Dr Fieser falls asleep at last and dreams of unburnt faces,
When gold medals are won by the ton for forgetting about
                                      the different races,
                                      God Bless America.

When in the Latin shanties the scented priesthood suffers
                                      metempsychosis
And with an organ entry *tutti copula* the dollar uncrosses
Itself and abdicates, when the Pax Americana cuts its losses
And a Pinkville memorial's built in furious shame by Saigon's
                                      puppet bosses,
                                      God Bless America.

When they can be happy without noise, without knowing where
                                      on earth they've been,
When they cease to be intellectual tourists and stop
                                      wanting to be clean,
When they send their children to bed at the proper time and
                                      say just what they mean,
And no longer trust the Quarterly Symposium and the Vicarious
                                      Screen,
                                      God Bless America.

When they feel thoroughly desolated by the short-haired Christ
> they pray to,
When they weep over their plunder of Europe stone by stone,
> releasing Plato
And other Freshman Great Books, when they switch off their
> Hoover and unplug Nato,
Pulling the chain on the CIA and awarding *Time* a rotten
> potato,
> *God Bless America.*

When qua-birds, quickhatches and quinnets agree at last to
> admit the quail,
When Captain Queeg is seen descending from the bridge as
> small and pale
As everyone else, and is helped with sympathetic murmurs
> to the rail,
When the few true defenders of love and justice survive to
> tell the tale,
> *Then, perhaps then, God Bless America.*

Riddle

What can she be? Can you guess? You should do, it's really
> quite easy.
Seek her familiar taste with the soft machine in your bone box.
Most of your life's involved with the murderous name she's
> hiding,
Mockingly putting her nose beside an upright finger,
Secret and smug, and knowing you know her dark intentions,
Knowing you know her real and wilful desire to trap you.

Should you say: 'Look, I am trying to read. So please go
> away now.'
Do you imagine that, edgy with print, you've a chance of
> succeeding?
Into the house she drags her unused power like a satchel,

Carelessly breaking your minutes, laughing and sweeping
                                    the pieces
On to your spotless boredom: one glance is enough to undo you,
Sitting in failing light with your endless fear of the cold cook.

Think what the finest mind, his wild hair streaming with silver,
Think what the wistful mind in the end is bound to feel like:
Nobody comes all day. Nobody comes to see him.
Nothing to do but hum and play with his *arbor vitae*.
Opens his beans at five with a steel rhinoceros opener,
Aching for wakeful nights, the dragon upon St George.

Pillow Talk

Wondered Knob-Cracker at Stout-Heart:
'Are you timed by your will, does your pulse
List credit, ready to slam like a till?
Can you keep it up?'

Growled Beard-Splitter to Smug:
'Your forces delay, bibbing at Northern walls
While snow drives rifts between, barring the way.
I am sufficient.'

Pleaded Knob-Cracker with Fail-Safe:
'You've boarded at last, your hands in your pockets,
Hat on the back of your head and flags up the mast.
Can't I come with you?'

Nodded Beard-Splitter to Sorrowful:
'The islands are prisons and no one returns,
No power or possessions where my rule is.
I will make you mine.'

All the Members of My Tribe are Liars

Think of a self-effacing missionary
Tending the vices of a problem tribe.
He knows the quickest cure for beri-beri
And how to take a bribe.

And so the mind will never say it's beaten
By primitive disturbance of the liver:
Its logic will prevent its being eaten,
Get it across the river.

But faced with this assured inconsequence
That damns the very method that is used,
It leaves the heart unproselytized and hence
Admits that it's confused.

I know I'm acting, but I still must act.
I melt to foolishness, and want it ended.
Why it continues is this simple fact:
I'd hate to end it.

For now the jungle moods assert their terms
And there's no way to check them if they lie:
The mind attempts to solve the thing, but squirms
And knows exactly why.

The world is everything that is the case.
You cannot see it if you are inside it.
That's why the tortoise always wins the race:
The very terms decide it.

I cannot help it if I am contented
With being discontented that I falter:
That's why psychology was first invented
So that we needn't alter.

It is a strange position to be in.
It would be different if I didn't know
Why the unlikely animal should win,
Which cannibal should row.

You'd think there'd be a way of cutting out
Those self-destructive layers of introspection.
To reach the truth at last without a doubt
Of making the connection.

That's why the missionary, on his guard,
Is wondering why the cannibal's so merry,
And why it is so very very hard
To be a missionary.

Star Bestiary

Lacerta
I finger the portals of some strange event,
Unseeing,
The watcher.

Cygnus
From beam to beam, extended and powerful,
My neck soft,
The weeper.

Lyra
No matter what escapes me,
At the centre, the recorder,
The dream.

Vulpecula and Anser
Meanwhile at the back gate
With stuffed grinning mouth and silent paws,
The crime.

A Footnote to Ovid

Arbor eris certe mea (Metamorphoses, I)
Run slowly now. And I won't follow faster.
Let me without pursuit catch up with you.
Or if my question fails, go on, go on,
But slower now. For see, it puzzles you,
You put down roots into my patient ground.
The tree stirs, seems to be saying yes:
Art is appeased. The slim girl running still.

The Choir Master

Alkman, Seventh Century BC
Oh my sweet girls, dear girls, with your so clear round voices
Linked in the sounds I taught you, your eyes on the page
And all the air no Siren struck with such compulsion
Alive in my ear like the breath of our own Kalliope
Without whose favour dance is graceless, no song moving,
Whose name is always on my lips, and is your name
My dears, as I urge you on like horses to your goal.

Now my legs fail me, standing in the colonnade
Clutching my black heart. If only I could be a bird!
An unharmed gazed-at bird, the colour of distant water,
A bird not alone but flying in easy neighbourhood,
A noble cormorant or tilted migrant gull,
Each far wave bursting for a moment into flower,
Oh my singing pupils, flowers of the sea's same song!

I am old. Your hands slip into mine for friendship
And you sing of the new life, all that I cannot teach.
For there are three seasons: summer and winter, and autumn
is three,
But in the new life when buds come there is no satisfaction,
Fruit and harvest, none, and no store. Spring is an ache,

In spring the mountains break down and weep, the snowdrop
Turns away, heavy with grief. And I clutch my heart,

My heart which is like spring lightning in the mountains when
A lantern is dashed to the ground and the gods roar with
                                                    laughter.
In my dream I am rooted and a witness, amazed and curious:
They bring a simple dairy churn, though cast in gold,
And you, my dears, fill it yourselves with the milk of a lioness!
And proceed to turn out a monstrous cheese which Hermes
                                                    himself
Might well have had appetite for after he'd murdered Argos!

Ah well, my own tastes are simple enough. Something like
                                                    porridge
Suits me now. You I've groomed and coaxed, my dear sisters,
It's no wonder your skills and beauty astound me still,
As hooves, as wings. You think me an old owl chunnering
In an attic, perhaps, or dare I hope as a ship's pilot
As we steer with one voice like a swan on the streams of
                                                    Xanthus,
Oh my dear girls, Kalliope's daughters, my daughters, my
                                                    music.

London Songs

   1 Missing
Lonely in London is an endless story,
Tired in the sun on the District Line,
With Baron's Court baked beans opened in Ealing,
Tossing in bed and staring at the ceiling,
And: 'Yes, Mr Holdsworth, I'll put you through.'
A lot of work and not much glory
And a letter to Mum that says you're fine.

You played me songs on your piana.
Its E was missing like a tooth.

It always rained when I came to see you,
Rained like the mint, the window creaked with rain.
You sat in the window and I told you the truth.

Lonely in London is an endless story.
Where did you go to? Who do you see?
I played at being with you, yes I'm sorry.
Now in this dog's soup I'm less than me,
Miss you, your piana, your piana and your cardigan,
Miss you on Friday, miss you on Monday,
Your cardigan, your tears and the baked-bean smells.
You're like a secret that nobody tells,
Lonely in London, somewhere, now.

2 Dusk

Rain on the river, and this hour of dusk
Settling slowly, imposingly, on London
As though its greatest shopwalker has died
Like a pianist about to play Busoni,
Hands resting in waxen contemplation
In white cuffs quietly upon his knees,
And women, weeping pearls, are gathered now
In Bond Street as the black discreet cortège
Rumbles slowly down to Piccadilly.

Rain on the river, and this hour of dusk
Settling on a city inventive of pleasure,
Secure in pleasure, in its terrible pleasure.

3 Fruit Machine

In love I take my chances,
In love I eat my greens,
Too old for idle glances
I live beyond my means:
I've tried the dogs and dances,
And now it's fruit machines.
From New Cross Gate to Deptford
The fruit is spinning fast,

And as I range I save my change
And make the bitter last.
Oh it's cherries and bells on Friday,
On Sunday plums and pears,
But pounds and jars and sevens and bars
Means whoops up the Saturday stairs.

The girls hang on my shoulder
To watch the fruit go round,
I may be getting older
But I certainly hold my ground,
And if it makes them bolder
I stand another round.
From New Cross Gate to Deptford
The beer is brown and deep,
Just a veal-and-ham and a Babycham
Will make the dollies leap.
Oh it's cherries and bells on Friday,
On Sunday plums and pears,
But pounds and jars and sevens and bars
Means whoops up the Saturday stairs.

The spinning fruit has woken
That child of dangerous charm
Who lures me with a token
And keeps me in alarm:
My envelope is broken
To pull his magic arm.
From New Cross Gate to Deptford,
Happily after dark,
When fruit falls thick I dance out quick
With a girl in Greenwich Park.
Oh it's cherries and bells on Friday,
On Sunday plums and pears,
But pounds and jars and sevens and bars
Means whoops up the Saturday stairs.

Cradle Lecture

They are the crooks-and-lugs of our future
Whose keyhole's baby shape is less than we want,
Miles more than we imagined, framing
A tilted scape of brushed lawns and pedestals
Twittering and aromatic in the evening light
Down which they run with slipping socks
To an invisible stream.

But they're linen-shopped still with their shucked toes
Beading the flat soft wedge of foot,
Their pudgy ancliffs and unstraightened knees.
Dear Nem, it is the privileged role of a father
To mumble in the beard you seize with such rapture,
Like prophetic rescuable finger-wagging Anchises
Who only staggers himself.

Lullaby

Sleep little baby, clean as a nut,
Your fingers uncurl and your eyes are shut.
Your life was ours, which is with you.
Go on your journey. We go too.

The bat is flying round the house
Like an umbrella turned into a mouse.
The moon is astonished and so are the sheep:
Their bells have come to send you to sleep.

Oh be our rest, our hopeful start.
Turn your head to my beating heart.
Sleep little baby, clean as a nut,
Your fingers uncurl and your eyes are shut.

The Father's Song

Dear girl, your bud unfolded
And brought you to this peace,
But my drab heart is still patrolled
By its corrupt police.

The past is eyeing hungrily
The future it denies,
And I look jealously upon
The angel in your eyes.

My body's single, and my love
A melancholy roar.
The children hide their faces when
I stand outside the door.

In dreams of the advances
Of loud uprooted trees,
I stand in quiet terror
While you sleep at your ease.

When men give birth to nightmares,
Their precious oil is spilt,
Yet love's enlarging waters guide
The voyage of his guilt.

Bound to the mast and deaf with shame,
He has to suffer much:
Dear child, hold in your little hands
His conscious, fatal touch.

And ride upon that jumart
Out of the sinking pit.
Hold the instant in your hands,
Oh bless and admonish it.

The Wreck

I

Ear hanging
Like a bat
Folds up its fears
In what it hears,
Though sound bring
A distant violence,
Channels the silence
Like a shot.

Eye imperilled,
Live opal,
By knives of nature,
Dangerous feature,
Love's milled
Unissued money,
Dark honey
For pale people.

Mouth compulsive
Fastened to love,
Its one mission
Shaping passion,
Talking to live
By its own sound,
With what it found
Still alive.

Brain disordered
Into hope,
Fertile with hair,
Pianism, sheer
Breath, shed
Of much fact,
Only the act
And its shape.

Hand calmest,
Fashioning,
That once was gill,
Horror in well
That were best
To be understood
A source of good,
A form of song.

2

Fingers might force
A firm descent
From neck's trap,
Uplifted face
And parted lip,
From hair at nape
And spine's tent.

But slow smile
Is held instead,
Your eyes look
Hopeful to small
Birds over the wreck,
Too much awake,
The moment dead.

3

It holds us here
Rapt in unfair
Staggered lives
Where nothing moves
But is changed
And our fringed
Instruments
Get few hints,
Give few: and we
Have no way.

Love's widow
It had no shadow,
Hurt to be cut
It suffered that,
Developed phases
And different sizes
The way a mountain
Can maintain
A melted profile,
Titans refuel.

Its days are returning
Without warning,
With garden smile,
Hello to snail,
With stubborn bent
And pollen count,
With frozen hair
And flannel cure,
With long hike
Or with rake.

In the end
There is no land.
We speak from systems
Respecting customs,
With good throw
And follow-through
Relax on green,
Or shocked at pain
In warm wicker
On half-acre.

When tilting plank
Suggests we sink,
To cry stop
Is out of step.

Fledglings shrivel
On dusty gravel
Where high bird
Cries hard
All day, all night,
Too late, too late.

4
On level lawns
Where hidden worms
Are inching under,
In bruised half-light
The wet bowls slide,
Machines for thunder,
And players move
In attitudes
Of pitch and balance
As though to free
Astronomy
Of human talents.

This dance is love
And lids alive
Direct the pattern
Of the half-felt
Still intellect
And lurching Saturn:
The centre holds
As the game rolls
Whose woods are liars,
And life enfolds
With all its hopes
Our aching bias.

5
Imagination
Link and star
Assume your station,

Let your far
Light of the brain
Become a part
Of the whole chain
That holds the heart
And keeps it calm
Immaculate
From every harm
The eyes create.

Only the mind
Can liberate
Desires we bind
To body's state:
Mortality,
Intent to please,
Is governed by
Admired disease
And vulnerable
Creatures sigh
As in its pull
They seek to die.

A living bloom
Falls from the fire
To light the room
While we admire
Shadows of flame
That touch the ceiling
Losing our name
With the same feeling,
Alert and chaste,
That the small deer
Alice embraced
Felt without fear.

And still it dies,
But in the air

There seems to rise
A shadow where
The senses fought
And won their prize,
Where love has caught
Complexities
Of shaping death
And passed beyond
The double breath
Of being fond.

Forget the hours:
Summer has gone
And clocks are flowers
To blow. Look on
The laden touch
Of brow and wrist
As showing such
As are not kissed
How clearly might
The senses play
Out of our sight
And far away.

6

Now by a window
Reflected in air
Or in rain's mesh
Or framed sash
Pictured there.

Long after light
The forgiven riot
With its mastery
Of history
Is perfect quiet.

Over distances
Too great to kiss,
The mind's aim
Of striking home:
Easy to miss.

It lodges here
Without sorrow
In love's dream,
Is still time
Until tomorrow.

Tomorrow, we say,
When we yield
And give battle,
Tomorrow will settle:
Tomorrow, healed.

7

Above the lake
The peaks in line,
Roped by the book
And measured rain,
Knuckle on arrow,
Welcome in stone
Our slippered hike
From hidden forms
Of barking farms
To open narrow
And tilted plain.

The space between
Our eyes is drunk,
Legs are in line
And the hands link
As clouds unslacken,
Changing the bank
All afternoon

Where bouncing shape
Of knitted sheep
Disturbs a bracken
Like old ink.

You last men
Who mind the map
Will shelter an
Uncertain hope:
Forgotten song
Can make you weep
And fail to win
The backward praise
Of future's prize,
Slither along
The gradient's slip.

We have your lack
And have it ever
As a thrown stick
Falls to the river,
An endless story,
Asking no favour
Wading to wreck
Nothing answered
All unsaid,
A promontory
To look over.

Dear bellied earth
Hangs at the edge
Of despair's path,
The bad cells lodge
In favourite valleys,
Raving the ridge
And curtained heath
Of withdrawn state,
With pain in sight,

Fearing its malice,
Its turned-down badge.

Our miniature's
Your memory,
Your death is ours
Going your way.
Heart is beating
At open view:
A mountain's laws
Impress the species
As being spacious,
A useful meeting,
A way to go.

And is much more,
Is love, its breath
That climbers share
In being both.
The landscape yawning
Hides a truth
We are quite near,
But trolls and pooks
On misty peaks
Whisper their warning
To find the path.

From distant ice
Fell finds its fall,
Water the peace
Of perfect will
And we the weather
Of being well,
Lifting the face
To the dangerous light
Of getting late,
Treading together,
The instep full.

The Silent Woman

What does she see?
What has it taught her?
Fire in the tree,
Leaves on the water.

What has it taught her,
Child of the heart?
Leaves on the water
Break apart.

Child of the heart,
When talking islands
Break apart
Your simple silence,

When talking islands
Turn away,
Your simple silence
Has nothing to say.

Turn away
My dear: their chatter
Has nothing to say,
Little matter.

My dear, their chatter
Is only fear,
Little matter
Who can hear.

Is only fear,
The body's quiet
Who can hear
The sap's riot,

The body's quiet
Possessing the tree,
The sap's riot
Silently

Possessing the tree.
Her days grow shorter
Silently.
Leaves on the water,

Her days grow shorter.
What does she see?
Leaves on the water,
Fire in the tree.

The Labours of Hercules

I

I did all that I had to do, for you
Exacted like a shadow every part
Of the compelling bargain. At the start,
With all the brashness of the strong and new,
I vowed to see the hateful business through.
I tried to learn my destiny by heart
And shape my future like a work of art
As though your pressing cries were real and true.

My deeds were natural at least. They kept
On being found out, though they always hid,
Like animals whose shelters that they make
Show the devourer where they lately slept.
I raged. I boasted. Undid what I did,
And what I did was nothing, some mistake.

2

And what I did was nothing, some mistake
On which there had to be a compromise
Since you were weak by virtue of my size
And only your demands could make me quake.

But you were not to spy nor I to fake.
I could not hesitate, retort, advise,
And you could never flatter or tell lies.
There was too much for both of us at stake.

Did the gods envy us this contract, then?
And did they visit on the hero, curled
Still inside his shell, the double snake?
Who killed them both? And O who sobbed out when
Their flat skins like a fable showed a world
Where time was drilled and matter kept awake?

3

Where time was drilled and matter kept awake,
Where danger crawled into a door and soon
Stood upright on its shadow, where the moon
Dropped lions which with an idle bite could take
A finger off, as little girls eat cake,
One pair of eyes watched through an afternoon
Across the stones and sand where bones were strewn
For the appointed lord they could unmake.

Squatting in silence I could almost hear
Bored laughter from the clouds. I seized a tree,
Uprooted it, and made my peace. I slew
That ordinary shape that was my fear
And found that I could walk upright and free
Beneath a careless and impartial blue.

4

Beneath a careless and impartial blue,
Beyond the friendly hills of childhood, lay
A second mystery, and in its way
The only mystery to which was due
The courtesy of genuine struggle. Few
Had ever come back from that squelching fray
Where the strange beast in bracken, mist and clay
Rose as it had to, did what it must do.

Again, again, again, again, again,
Again, again, again! I felt to hunt
Those lurching heads through their organic glue
Brought small relief, for you lay panting then,
And of the cost were blankly ignorant,
And only my achievement really knew.

5

And only my achievement really knew
What lay beyond their stink, and what the third
Pursuit and the most sacred was. I heard
A different voice in that subsiding brew,
Small voice of sighs. With horns of golden hue
It lifted nostrils of alarm and stirred
The cold air with its breath. I knew no word
To tell me where it was, or what, or who.

I think you understood, and we conspired
To lure that creature from the freedom that
Defined its beauty, flickering in the brake.
And there was nothing. And I was too tired
To cry it was not my fault all fell flat:
What it was for was only for your sake.

6

What it was for was only for your sake
And your desire. You wanted what was lost,
Thundered to greet it like the horns that tossed
A favourite. In ignorance we break
What we love most. That was the hollow ache
That haunted me unkindly as I crossed
To the fourth labour where through drift and frost
I tracked it like a thirst I had to slake.

How strange the impulse captured in the ice!
It carries many frozen loves. It steers
Them hairy still and gaping, half-opaque,
To my unwilling strength, the spoiling price

Of my perception, paid for with warm tears,
Dragged from my existence like a lake.

7

Dragged from my existence! Like a lake
Around which bathers test its clarity
With toes and leave it muddied, I was free
Of your bad dreams until you tried to shake
Me into them because you could not wake.
How deep they were! I shuddered at your plea
To cleanse you of them: it was not for me.
And yet for you I took up brush and rake.

This was the fifth and foulest. And deformed.
It seemed the weakness of the endless giver
To do it just because you asked me to.
Yet strong in this as always, I performed
The idle deed like a diverted river
Brought senseless in to its admirer's view.

8

Brought senseless in to its admirer's view
The living brain seemed greenish and disused,
Pulsating slightly, shiny, apple-bruised:
This too was dreaming, for the silent queue
Of mourners shuffling to the ill-lit pew
Turned and showed us beaks, screamed and refused
To sing. I tried to catch them, but amused
They wet the floor and tried to fly. And flew.

This sixth was for the birds, but not to lose
Is only one prerequisite of winning.
The brazen fancies fall as they are hit,
But you are always there to make me choose,
And as you governed me from the beginning
So we shall never see the end of it.

9

So we shall never see the end of it:
Without your needs I've nothing to be bold
About; without my arm you're uncontrolled.
Together as that thread in fat we fit,
Dark soft and clear, hot in its narrow pit.
But when we walk, my dear, we are unrolled,
A solid shape and hard, so white and cold
We burn out energy when we are lit.

After the seventh, something I had complained
About, colossan on the sands, you lied:
'The dual freedom of the three-legged pair.'
Chained to the path we tread and yet not chained,
We trust each other not to step aside
Since our continuing is what we share.

10

Since our continuing is what we share,
Come with me then! Our running daughters clean
The grains in air. The breakers gasp. We mean
Only what we mean. Skin strains. Birds scare
Above a chequered hill of shouting where
The happy ugly family, unseen
By gods and suchlike, feasts upon the green,
And they, and light, have everything to spare.

The eighth is easiest. Something to do
With death, implacable, yet of a kind
That seems to soothe: 'You do not have to die.'
As though one drunken meeting makes it true
That no one of authority will mind
When we contrive our parting by and by.

11

When we contrive our parting by and by,
My dear, the desert will be there to hand:
Not as you might imagine, a dead land

D

Where nothing's coloured, trees don't even try,
Where water is uninvited, where birds sigh,
Flapping like tents over impermanent sand.
Not dead, but without meaning; rich, unplanned.
Not dead but mad, mad to the single eye.

Nine times we have mewed our triumph: now
Something is really up. The scenery
Closes like an album and we sit
Knowing the why at last but not the how.
We shiver slightly now. When both are free
It will not matter which of us has quit.

12

It will not matter which of us has quit,
Though now I know (perhaps knew all along)
Which of us finally would prove the strong:
Not me. Into my vice-like grip your grit
Curled its opacity until I split.
My harmony foundered beneath your song
(Ten for the ten contentments; not for long)
With all the discipline of licensed wit.

Home, herds: you are a thin posterity,
The generations' pleasure. Like a stray
I stumble righteously back to my lair,
And left pretending that I cannot see,
Caring immensely, no, I will give way
For no one, left pretending not to care.

13

For (no one left) pretending not to care
Becomes an academic exercise:
I could as easily hold up the skies
As sit here writing in a summer chair
Or find that voluntary garden where
I can assert my title to the prize
That's mine if I unravel the disguise,
That doubleness we live in as in air.

I do care. Even at the eleventh hour
One has to hope for a miraculous birth,
Though from the golden tree the dragons sigh
Who have the whole of life within their power,
Who will yield nothing. And the widowed earth
Will sit there bravely smiling and not cry.

14

Will sit there bravely smiling? And not cry?
Yes, even so, the heroes gone at last
Who were the only status of a past
That bored us all and lied compulsively
Though we all knew it really had to lie.
We honour it in memory, though fast
The memory goes, new words to learn, new cast:
New how, new when, new where, new what, new why.

And on the stroke of twelve, the twelfth deed done,
As I return now from the shapeless dead
And the final dog, let me with calm review
All my great failures, sum them up in one,
And above all, my dear, let it be said
I did all that I had to do for you.

15

I did all that I had to do for you,
And what I did was nothing, some mistake
Where time was drilled and matter kept awake
Beneath a careless and impartial blue,
And only my achievement really knew
What it was for, was only for your sake
Dragged from my existence like a lake,
Brought senseless in to its admirers' view.

So we shall never see the end of it
Since our continuing is what we share:
When we contrive our parting by and by

It will not matter which of us has quit,
For no one left pretending not to care
Will sit there, bravely smiling, and not cry.

Scenario for a Walk-on Part

The borrowed walking-stick that makes me lame,
The single curiously worn-down tyre,
The hanging button and forgotten name,
The grinning of the vulnerable liar:
These are the gambits of a chosen game,
A well-cut personality on hire,
Mirrors too low, the eyebrows graze the frame,
Warming my hands before an unlit fire.

Dinner a skirmish, legs uncrossed and crossed,
An alp of linen and the sight of nylons,
Pudding arriving full of fruit and frost,
And, swimming in their syrup, smoking islands,
Lips at a silver spoon proclaim me lost,
My single joke counters a threat of violence.
The table cleared, I cannot count the cost
Of dinner or of nerves. The rest is silence.

Now in the sharpest lock at close of day,
Hands as if manacled, the gravel spurting,
My hosts with linked arms waving me away,
The gulf of what I didn't say still hurting
(Since you are only known by what you say),
Yawning beneath my silent murmur skirting
The dangerous excuse, the wish to stay,
Like the evasions of protracted flirting:

Alone I drive away with my awareness
That once again I've failed the magic word
Whose demon locks me up inside my bareness,
The charming openness unsaid, unheard.

Is love the better for its hurts and rareness?
I frown and think so. Falling into third
On a hill, I glimpse a face: the sheer unfairness
Fights with my sense of shame at being stirred.

The sexy minister reclaims his scarf,
A girl in denim runs to meet a train,
Mrs Jocasta bastes the fatted calf,
The guests have taken to their beds again:
I hold the floor but nobody will laugh,
No one is there to kiss if I complain,
I enter only in the second half,
Unwilling, underwritten, used to pain.

Her Morning Dreams

I trail in my sculpted sheets to the misty window
And rub a patch there like a liquid bruise.
Yes. Stooping in blue. Propped bicycle.

But absence is your only sort of news.
Over the toast and the slit boring letters
The damp end flares in ribbons like a fuse.

What do I think? Do I think it matters?
Do I think what matters? Do I think?
Oh yes, I think. Don't worry, you wouldn't notice.

The unmade bed. Finger on my pink.
Dead as he groaned upon a linen ocean,
Who would have thought he had such little ink?

Dreams for you. The head is cut in walking.
Sour puffballs. Silence. Clouds of dust.
It's a bad day for any sort of singing.

I thought that you were someone I could trust.
I can begin. Well, I can try beginning
If only somebody will say I must.

Are you my pal? Are you Ardent Ardvaark?
At first I took you for the kind who while
He sobs sinks fangs, while he sings does murder

In blue clothes, greets with insinuating smile
Across the gravel with his hands extended
In preacher or in nightclub singer style

Under a pained yet cheerful load of welcome.
Now you are someone in my morning dreams.
I was so bored that summer. Can you imagine

Life shrunk and wrinkled to its seams,
Its hopes on threads, its memories in pockets,
The sluggish mouth disowning all its streams?

Can you imagine the clean shock of naming,
And love acknowledging its paradigm?
With you misery had as little meaning

As backfriends to fingers galloping in time
With the Catalan pupil of the Neapolitan master,
Each note as true as an expected rhyme.

Perhaps you never meant that sort of magic,
Perhaps the fault was mine, grateful allure
Scoring a million in the cheated darkness,

Pretending the experience was pure.
God help us, darling, aren't we only human?
Kiss me again and let's be really sure.

I believe all disasters now, believe all pain.
As for your life, however much you hate it,
However bad it smells upon your bed,

You simply cannot go back and create it:
Something will tell you that you have to cry,
Something will tell you this was always fated.

So I have tried beginning. Or is it ending?
Things I remember cover me with shame,
They linger obstinately every morning.

Stupid. But every day it is the same.
And nothing felt like that is ever final.
Not you. Not me. Nobody is to blame.

Dreams. You walking down a dusty pavement.
Your head is always strangely turned away,
Carried as though bandaged, with little movement.

Now is the time to say it: nothing to say.
You came and went with carefully rolled forearms.
You held life in their empty space that day.

I pad from bed to stove to fill a pan.
Sometimes a step is just a step too far:
No time to think what it has got you into.

Even the job of knowing where you are
Becomes a full-time dangerous occupation.
It's honey at the bottom of the jar

But no one can be sure until it's eaten.
Not everything is right. What's possible?
I pull the whole drawer of my mind down on

My foot. Hell. The cat's beneath the bedspread
Like a blister, showing that you have gone.
I walk from room to room, trying the answer:

One from two is wrong, and one from one
Is neater. Morning dreams are calmer weeping.
All my indignities spill from the sun.

Listen to it now. All night like wedded chaos.
The creeper's down, the storm makes such a fuss.
Trying to count the blows of rain is useless.

I shall sit it out, here by the misty glass,
Till I can face the morning's empty graces,
The window sill become an abacus.

Aberporth

Sky is performing feats of weather over
Hills wooded to the top, humped private hills
Whose birds look down not up. Briar's between
The fields: he keeps the eating sheep from knowing
What's on the other side. Beneath the path
A culvert runs, hidden for fifty years:
Some work will dig it up again.

Yes, nature is incurious, we know.
The butterflies as big as prayerbooks draw
No lesson from the india wings they thumb through,
While chapel slate aches with its uglification
Of primrose and violet, and the gold-black graves
Make even death elaborate and absurd
Like a bad conjuror.

The sea is much visited here, whose colours are cooler
And life uncertain as well it might be in
The earth's tears. Gulls on the sand look sharp.
Without anxiety the jellyfish is hideously still,
And the same could be said of the cliffs where wind carries
The loves of freewheeling crickets across a haze
Of sun-baked blackberries.

But we so easy are still not at our ease:
Such closeness open to us as though to a
Laconic Christ, hands flat to the ears with pity!

How we wish not to judge, wish for the starlight
And its emblems, the foliage globose and witchy,
With sounds coming nearer (Frrr! Frrr!) speaking
Of something that might content us.

Ghost Village

Something takes me away, even from the spotlit
Indian clubs of our small happy government,
The gasp of hope and memory's applause,
In brown rooms, in yellow rooms, in red rooms by the sea,
To the colourless and soundless world we half-remember.

Presaged and annotated by our paltry sobs,
Older than all the lives we know or ever knew,
So sharply critical of the success of matter,
Keeping its own activities a deadly secret,
It is blind and alert as the black eyes of negatives.

Something said somewhere at some time is not enough
To appease its absorbing interest in what we did not mean
To old friends suddenly noticed as they glance up from books
With the sort of look which asks nothing because it is not

                                                    worth it,
By the curled sea in rooms we shall half-forget.

Old friends in new rooms, new friends in old rooms:
It sees them come and go, because it is not worth it,
But a path down the valley cracked with grass
Brings us to the ghosts who must be faced,
Who questioned the blind world and would not let it lie.

Ghosts have hunters, but the hunters lose the track,
For the craned neck does not suspect a reply
And the star or the heron is never asked if it requires
To be looked at, by those who glance up from books
When the curtains are drawn back from the evening sky.

Friendless, rootless by choice, they made a home for this bay
Where pairs of stone windows were set to frown at the sea
With all the gloomy unconcern of self-absorbed exiles
Whose delineation of the jealousies and dribbled ghylls
Only betrayed their real longing and peculiar laughter.

Did neighbours wonder at the striding, the leaping of gates?
Did Squire Tribute, coming from beyond the ridge
Where the harnessed pismire superb in its plumes of dust
Pretended to be a horse on a careless errand,
Judge? Or was it changed, the outside world?

When Mistress Tidings courted Sinful the Silent
And whispers sent sidling three sides of the square
Returned across the gap, shocked and delighted,
Was it too much like what had always been known
To make much sense, the inside world?

For we have known that difference as well,
Hands drumming impatiently on green baize
As we listen to the next to last report,
The tank brimming, the wipers running freely,
Set for the coast and the foul pinks of love.

They took the mountain for its broken counterpart.
Steamers visited the creaking pier and the washed gravel
Lay heaped like wheat on the shore of their closed lives.
In front rooms hands were folded on knees. A ticking clock
Enlarged the stone silences, defining a central gravity.

They saw the cow turn her tail into a handle,
Replenishing three or four fields beside a cliff,
And resolved as they walked alone at evening in watchchains
To make their lives acceptable to others, their deaths
Only to themselves. And the fields steamed with joy.

Their children were the first to make shy advances,
Wove with fingers, were pinioned, wept, touched,

Cruelly accused the unhappy of being only unhappy,
Talked incessantly of the marriage of headland and valley
And thought of nothing much to say, but learned to read.

Until one day these became themselves the brooding exiles,
The best cap square set or the downed pick at noon,
The mountain unshaped with interjections of dynamite,
Tired of responsibility, dreaming, easily wounded,
Crying out to be, and being, successfully lured by cities.

Nothing is changed, and most of the dancing is still glum
In neighbouring villages where they watch and wait
For the silver band to assemble in the Sunday dusk.
Nothing is changed, when wishes are fulfilled
And again we stare into the boiling centre.

Nothing is changed, but everything will alter
And the blind world exults as we expect it should
Over the first and last, the inside and the outside,
The forms and secrets, friends and generations,
Pacts made by ghosts that some of us have tried to love.

So thinking, a tiny swivelling figure in the bay,
Hands in pockets, turning over stones with a holiday foot,
Posed between the unravelling tides and the abandoned houses,
Made an uncertain gesture, ceased watching the sea,
And plodded up the hill for company.

The Elms

Air darkens, air cools
And the first rain is heard in the great elms
A drop for each leaf, before it reaches the ground.
I am still alive.

Annotations of Giant's Town

1

Living in the air
Sleeping anywhere
Sheep are known to fall
But safe behind the wall
Cutting a fine edge
On outcrop or ledge
Gone if I look twice
Stones black with ice
Groan beneath my feet
Or make a cold seat
Storms come like love
Are level not above
Far is down not high
Tiny to the eye
Shining to the west
Wrinkled fishes nest
Blinking in the sun
Living is begun

2

Height dizzies me
And what I see
Standing in his palm
At the end of his arm
That is our fort
Is beneath thought
Miserable track
Trees folded back
Sea's lazy licking
Thin picking
Fin and feather
Out of the weather
Shouting defiance
Loud nonsense
Cloud stuff

From having enough
Come out of stone
Height is alone

3
Summer was his table
Eating what we were able
Sweet berry and grass
Cattle run in the pass
That will not meet their owner
Fool that is their donor
Who let them run away
Now we can eat all day
Cow-milk that we squeeze
Dripping into cheese
Ripping her fat sire
Out of the turning fire
Doubtful of our luck
Having bones to suck
Saving something for
The greed we can't ignore
Hugging us to death
Summer is his breath

4
Once by work of frost
Rocks split and were lost
Fox hid in their boulders
Fur-smells on shoulders
Stirred memory of fear
When alone and fox near
Then fox-fear and fox-coat
Settled at the throat
Met on the hill one night
Faces not in sight
Spaces behind the ears
Cold with fox-fears
Older without thought

Rambled beyond the fort
Scrambling down the scree
Knowing what to see
No more seeing what
Once seen and is not

5

Something happens there
Thunder in the air
Under a trickling stone
Where sheep have gone
Staring at his face
Or its liquid trace
For all above the hill
His expressions spill
This way and that
Careful as a cat
Hairs out on the neck
Ribbed like a wreck
Gibbering in the rain
Lightning like pain
Night closing in
Fur round the chin
Stirring of ember
Something to remember

6

Fear is no longer
When we grow stronger
Then the clean stranger
Is known danger
Visible and small
No longer tall
Whole bands at the border
Keep in order
Leaping from trees
Hear metal knees
Gear snatched away

Only the weak stay
Grown attached to death
Short of breath
Brought to some harm
By the timid arm
Die in his cage
Fear's hostage

7

Winter in the wood
Trees where they stood
Pleased to be seen
Though no longer green
Rowan and oak
Cut for smoke
Hut-warmth for songs
Fur and gongs
Stirring his tribute
With bared cubit
Pith and sour berry
To make us merry
Brew for love and him
For his unseen whim
Or for his pain
The cold come again
Luck running thin
Winter closing in